The Trick with Sticks

Author Linda Cawley

Illustrator Viktoria Wolf

RECOMMENDATIONS

"The story was inspired by the author's children and their struggles and triumphs to build friendships. It was initially written to help the author's children, but gradually, the story evolved into something I think would be helpful for ALL kids and parents. Oh, my goodness, the story is so clever. I teared up. Linda's got a Dr. Seuss style of writing, but her quality is beyond him, and so is her story. I wish I was a publisher, as I'd publish this on impulse! The images live on in my mind!"

Mark Le Messurier – Educator, Counsellor, Author, Public Speaker and Coach

"As a mother of ASD children, it is so wonderful to find a children's story so rich in opportunities to have deep, key conversations with all our children on the intricacies of social interactions. The Trick with Sticks unpacks the complex subject of making bonds with others and how to promote understanding, compassion and empathy for all of our children, inclusively. Bravo to Linda for this heartfelt, important story."

Cathy Domoney–Author and Mentor
<u>www.miraclereadymindset.com</u>

"In a time when our young people face so many social challenges, Linda Cawley is a Dr. Seuss for a new generation. Moving, authentic, poetic and practical, this book is for children, adults, and everyone in between. This poetic tale will inspire and resonate with those who feel lost with connection and finding their place, but it will touch something true and universal in all of us. I loved The Trick with Sticks *and would recommend it to everyone, especially to parents of children who are struggling with peers."*

Ingrid Freriks–MPsych (Clinical); BA(Hons) Psychology; MAPS. Clinical Psychologist, Family Therapist and Relationship Counsellor

"The Trick with Sticks is a beautifully told visualisation approach to explain the vastly complex nature of connection and friendship. With a focus on knowing your worth and value as a potential friend, it carefully highlights the unwritten rules of friendship for the consumer. The illustrations bring the profound messages presented in the book to life."

Autism SA

"This beautifully written and illustrated book provides personal insight into the challenges and complexities of navigating the social world. It is empowering and provides the reader with a gentle understanding of the importance of friendship, connecting with others and being accepted."

Caitlin Haines, Autism Spectrum Facilitator

"Wow! This educational story explores the challenges and successes of building and sustaining friendship bonds in a fun and thoroughly relevant way. Linda has incorporated aspects of other self-regulation-based strategies within the story, and she ties everything together in a seamless way. She has created a valuable resource not only for children, but for parents, teachers, and therapists alike."

Megan Tuckwell, Senior Occupational Therapist

For those who walk to the beat of their own drum

"There are ups

And there are downs

An adventure, a disaster?

I am in charge of my forever after"

Linda Cawley

PREFACE

So this all started one night with a box of matches! We were talking to our children about how certain behaviours affect friendships and how the bonds of friendship are created. We took the matches out of the box and started adding matches to piles for behaviours that contributed to friendships and took them away for behaviours that diminished friendships. Before we knew it, the behaviours that contributed to friendships had created a pile of matchsticks. We then had a conversation about the behaviours that took matchsticks away from the pile or behaviours which were effectively just orbiting the pile, neither contributing nor taking matches away. This matchstick analogy helped to visualise the tricks with friendships and so the idea of putting matches on your pile swirled around in my head until *The Trick with Sticks* was born.

This book has been designed so you can pick up the story at any point to discuss your child's day. You can hone in on the relevant part of the story, and relate their behaviour with a correlating behaviour and talk about what happens to the sticks. Ultimately this story is a tool to help your child recognise their behaviours and how they affect friendships.

©2020 Linda Cawley

All rights reserved. No part of this book may be used or reproduced by any means graphic, electronic or mechanical including photocopying, recording, taping or by any information storage retrieval system without written permission of the publisher except in the case of brief quotations embodied in critical articles and reviews.

ISBN 978 0 646 83040 7

The trick with sticks

My mother says to me

Is some are quick

And some are slow

Some will glow and some will blow

I search high, I search low

But wherever I go, how will I know

Why my friendships have highs and lows

Here I am, but far I am

They are there and I am here

I am here and they are there

Can anyone see me?

Can anyone hear me?

What shall I do?

I will figure this out!

What can I see?

What do they do?

Is there a secret weapon?

Is this some kind of magic?

Do I just need to do abracadabra?

I will watch

I will listen

I will be the magician

I will see how everyone gets into position

I can learn the tricks of the magican

I SEE IT!!!

Everyone has STICKS!!!

They are building

They are binding

They are bonding

They are winding

Anyone can pick up a stick

Everyone can choose

What they do with their stick

Will it go on the pile?

Will it be held for a while?

Or will it not ever see the pile?

What is this structure?

This magnificent structure

It is awesome, it is beautiful

It is a natural wonder

It withstands rain, hail and thunder

Just like a puzzle

The puzzle has pieces

They fit together

Everyone can have a piece

Piece by piece

One by one

Stick by stick

Together as one

There is something about them

They are different, but the same

Same but different

Different is ok

Same is ok

It is ok

OK?

I want to build

I want to play

I want to learn

I want to know how to put my sticks on the pile

There is a way for my stick to fit

What do I do, so it does not hit

Or go ka splat, ka split?

Or end up in a thousand bits?

There are ups

And there are downs

An adventure, a disaster?

I am in charge of my forever after

I will try to get the ball

Even if I fumble and fall

I will try to do my best

I will pass the test

My best, my best, my best

My teammates like my best

My stick goes in with the rest!

But if I think I can be slack

I will come down with a whack!

Only wanting to be a star

Not passing or looking for mates afar

My teammates will not like to play

My sticks will get taken away!

I will listen

I will pay attention

I will look you in the eye and answer your curious question

This takes practice and focus

My sticks go on the pile without hocus pocus!

But if I boast and only talk of myself

With no questions of anyone else

Make up lies to impress, it only ends up in a mess

My sticks will go from the pile

For them to go back, may take a while.

I will say hello

I will greet you with a smile

I will ask you how you are

You will think of me as a friend

Together we laugh and get excited

Together we cry if we are sad

Together we will help each other

Together we put our sticks on the pile

But if I look only at my feet

I walk straight past you in a beat

I don't see you, you don't see me

I will never know how wonderful you can be

You will never know the wonderful me

My sticks will never see the pile

You will never know my smile

I am cool, calm and collected

When things go wrong, I stay connected

I have many zones in my head

Blue, green, yellow and RED!

I stay cool, I put my sticks on the pile

I go with the flow, slow, I grow and now I glow

But if I blow

Like a volcano, I explode

Make a fuss and yell and scream

I can't see the need to be part of the team

It's my way or the highway

They stare, they get scared and run away

My sticks are taken, kicked and thrown away!

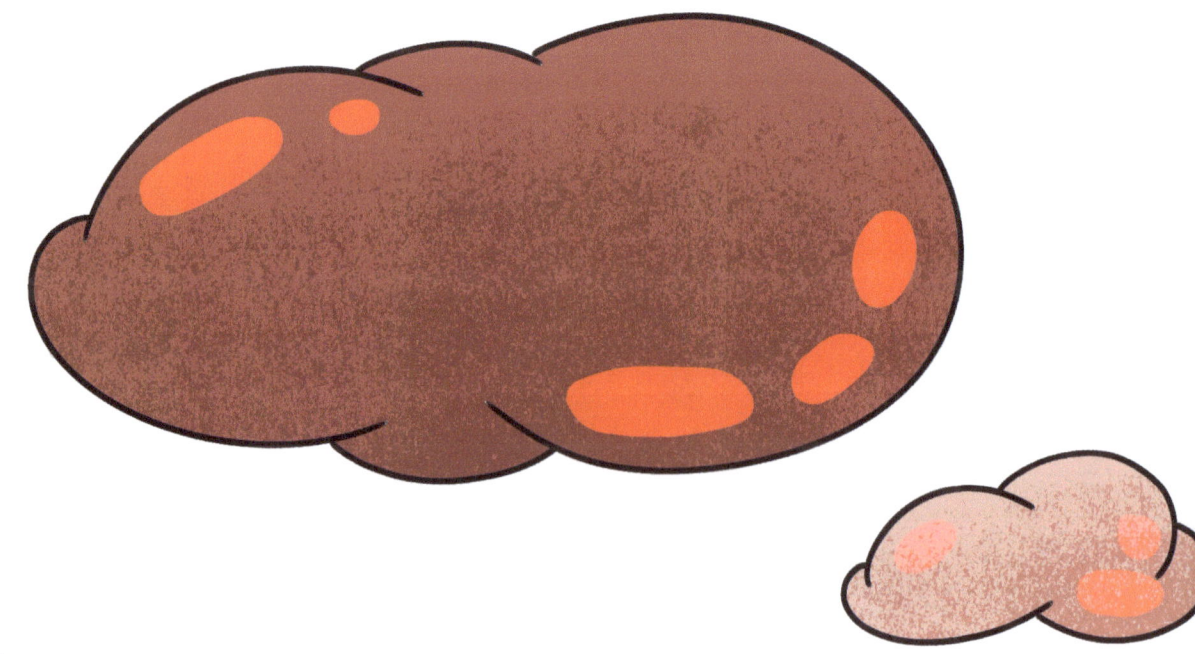

I am in the band

I play my sax

With all my heart, to the max

I practice, I am patient, I am no hack

I play in time

We all sound mighty fine

We are a team

They clap and cheer

We all beam

My sticks go on the pile, I gleam!

But if I let my mind wander

Not playing the same tune

Or playing the same beat

I am not being part of the team

They get annoyed and let off steam

My head is in the clouds

It is not the time to daydream

I need to be present

My sticks do not go on the pile, not today it seems

They are putting sticks on their piles

Their piles are getting bigger

Bigger and bigger

They gather, they play, they are each other's guest

They are loyal to their flock, they protect their nest

They never stop putting sticks with the rest

But, sometimes piles are mean

It seems

As hard as I try

They make me cry

I never feel part of the team

I am in a rut

But I listen to my gut

It is often right

I choose with all my might

Not to bite

To walk away

My stick is gladly given

My stick is worthy, it must be earnt

I take my stick for another day

Like a beautiful star

The sticks gather in a cluster

The bigger the cluster

The brighter they are

The closer they are

But if I only orbit that star

Never getting close, only afar

I will float like an astronaut, holding my sticks

I am on the outside looking in

I won't let go or pull any tricks

I want to join, I won't burn my sticks

I will keep trying to learn the trick with sticks

I will take a deep breath

I will be myself

The gravity will pull me, you see

Towards that bright, shining star

I will be part of the gang

Part of that beautiful stick cluster

My sticks are on the pile

I belong, I smile

Though sometimes it gets tricky

My wheels get a bit sticky

They won't turn, they yearn

For help, a nudge, a push to learn

Like a looming mountain

I start to climb

Up, up, up I go

Step by step

I start to sweat

I gasp for air

My throat is dry

I have a thirst

My lungs are about to burst

I persist, I resist the urge to give up

The top is near

I proceed, no fear

I keep a brave face

Keeping a steady pace

It is a hard road

Upwards I go

I am nearly there

A few more steps

I make it!

The view is spectacular!

I have come so far

I have learnt so much

No mountain will stop me

It is my conquest

Onwards I go

It is easier now

There are still bumps in the road

I still carry my load

But now I ride and try to glide

I choose my path

Where my line is cast

It happens so fast

Now I am having a blast!

My friendships take off

Everyone cheers and waves

Laughs and smiles

I feel warm, I feel comfortable

There is a sense of familiarity

Although venturing into the unknown

I feel I belong, I am happy being me

I am welcome, I relax, I smile

My sticks are part of the pile

My piles of sticks are pillars of strength

My mountain is but a molehill

My sticks are worthy, they are earnt and gladly given

My piles of sticks have laid a foundation

My sticks have built a skyscraper, a bridge, a rocket

My piles of sticks are beautiful clusters everywhere

The trick with sticks

Is knowing when

To make a choice

To choose a pile

To find a gem

A precious stone

To BE that gem

I will know when

I start MY piles

In my heart

I will be bold

My piles

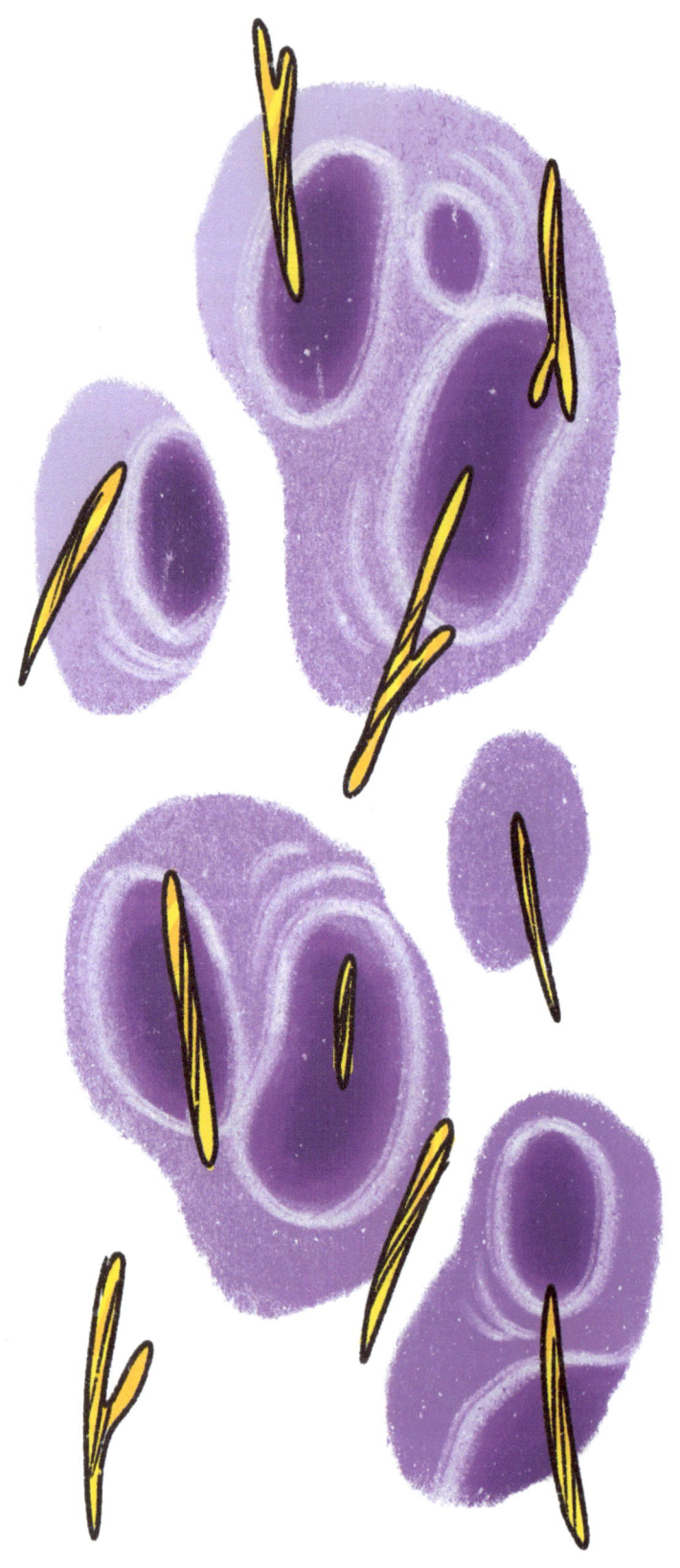

Will have friendships

Made of gold!

Go forth with one's stick

Like a lioness protecting her cubs

A firefighter dousing the flames

The tenacity of an industrious bee

I will be strong, I will be brave

I will just be

The wonderful me

It is a brave new world

Something different is needed

Sticks come in all colours

All shapes and all sizes

There is no limit to the number of piles

Like the universe, miles and miles

Something different, something new

Be brave, be bold

Imagine, create, anticipate

A new brew, a stew, a crew

A new super sticky, non-sticky glue!

I am building

I am binding

I am bonding

I am winding

I am part of this beautiful cluster

I can withstand rain, hail and thunder

I am my own natural wonder

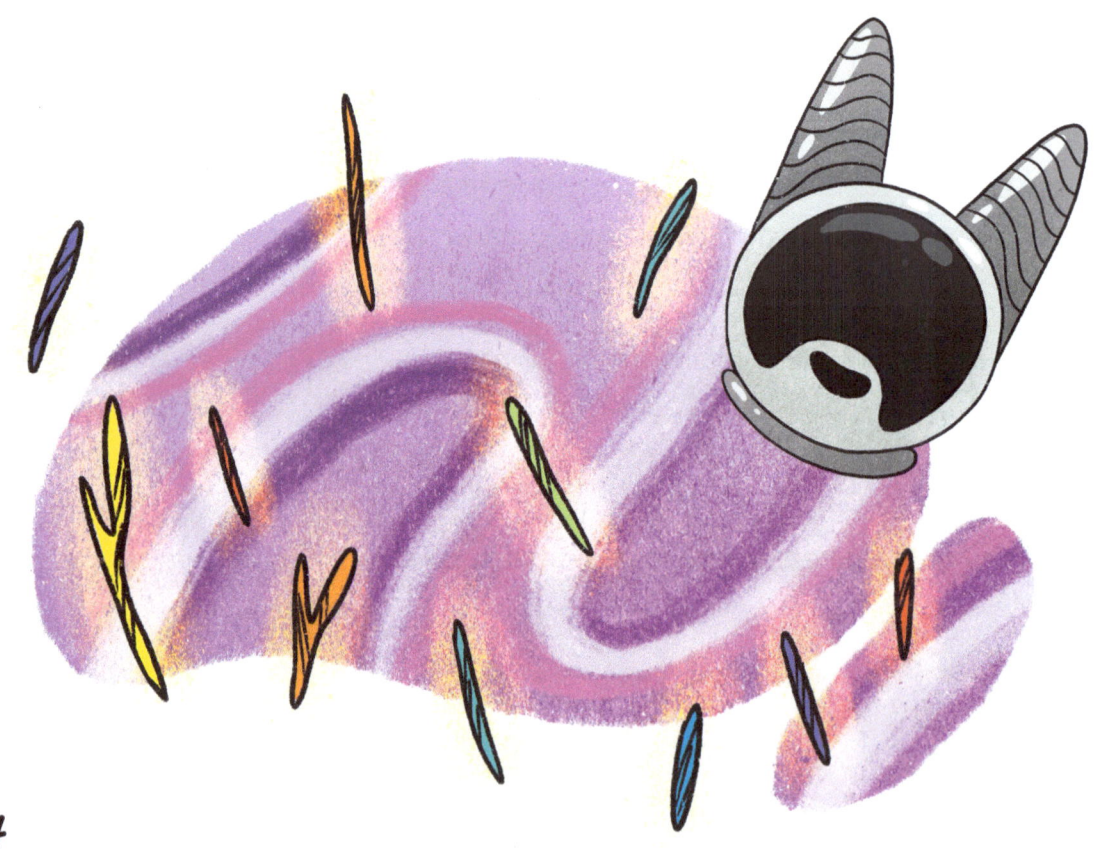

Stick by stick

Step by step

I have learnt the trick with sticks

I put sticks on the pile

I choose which pile

The piles go on for miles and miles

If my gut goes, "Uh-uh, no-go," then no

I start my own pile

I know my style

Others join my pile

I know the how to, when and why

I fly so high, past the sky

Nothing can stop me now, I know how

They are there and I am there

They are here and I am here

I go with the flow, now I glow

I go my own way and now I say

I have learnt the trick with sticks

I can muster myself into the cluster

I make choices, accept others no bluster

I have come so far, I am a STAR!

Different but the same

Same but different

Different is ok

Same is ok

It will be ok

Ok.

Dear Parents, Teachers and Carers,

I really hope you find this to be an uplifting story about self-worth, acceptance, happiness, and building confidence. It is a story that shows it is ok to be different, but most of all, it is a story that helps demystify friendships and the formation of bonds.

The Trick with Sticks is just one strategy to help children with friendships and bonds by creating a framework to understand and discuss social interactions. Friendships are a natural development process for most children, but there are some who find the development of friendships tricky. What draws children together? What keeps them together? What can parents, teachers or carers do to help children develop these friendships? What are these bonds, and how can they be explained?

There are many opportunities throughout the story for meaningful conversations, and the chance to reflect on the things that are happening in your child's life. This is so empowering for children who may be going through a tough time making friends or for a range of challenges, such as bullying, self-esteem, self-worth, unhappiness, low confidence and acceptance of themselves and others. This is highly recommended for children with autism spectrum disorder (ASD), as they can really struggle with friendships and often miss social cues or opportunities to connect, or they can make the same mistakes again and again. In addition to this, neuro-typical children often miss the clues on how to be inclusive and supportive of some of their friends, so this concept will empower everyone.

Parents often find it distressing to see their children struggling to interact or being left out. This distress is often heightened by a feeling of helplessness, with no clear framework to provide support or assistance to your child. If your child is struggling to fit in or getting bullied, or if your child is never invited to a birthday party, then this book is one way to help.

The Trick with Sticks teaches your child they cannot control what other children do; they can only control their own actions and behaviours. If they make changes to their actions and behaviours in a positive way, they will elicit positive responses from those changes. However, this also works in reverse. Negative actions and behaviours will elicit negative responses. There are also times when they might be orbiting groups without realising, and when they do this, they are neither forming bonds nor destroying them. However, this is a good space for your child to observe what others are doing. By watching and listening, they can learn while they are orbiting to help figure out what other children do.

I encourage you to start talking to your child about "putting sticks on their pile" as part of your everyday conversations. Each day, ask your child if they think they put any sticks on their piles. If they say yes, ask them what they did to put sticks on their pile. If there was a problem, ask what they think the consequence of their action or behaviour was by way of asking about what happened to their sticks.

The idea of "sticks on a pile" provides children with a means to visualise their progress, and it acts similarly as a rewards system, where they can see sticks being added or removed from the pile. Being a mental concept, it also encourages self-assessment and self-regulation, as nobody else can see the pile.

Continuous reinforcement of positive actions and behaviours will help your child to build those bonds, which will eventually form friendships. Discussing negative actions and behaviours will help your child to understand the consequences via what happens to the sticks. The sticks give your child a visual to help them understand how bonds can grow, and how actions and behaviours influence what happens to their sticks and their piles.

So go forth with your sticks and watch, help and guide your child to learn, grow and shine. May they learn the trick with sticks, and stick by stick, may they build their piles everywhere and at any time. There are no limits!

Linda Cawley

P.S. See if you can get your child to find the space helmet hidden in the story. It is only there when a particular dog appears! Which dog is it?

ABOUT THE AUTHOR

Linda Cawley lives in Adelaide, South Australia, with her husband, her teenage daughter, her tweenage son, the most tolerant dog in the world, Molly, and a growing, quite alarmingly large python.

Before writing her children's book, Linda completed a degree in business management, double majoring in Japanese from the University of South Australia. At the beginning of her career, she worked for Unilever, a multi-national, fast-moving consumer goods (FMCG) company, after which she started and built two companies with her husband, one a consultancy firm in 2002 and the other a tech start-up in 2015, while raising two children.

Linda loves to travel and learn about different cultures. Her love of travel has taken her to many places, with her favourite adventures taking her backpacking around Europe in the mid-90s on a $50-a-day budget with no mobile phone, working and living in Japan teaching English, and working as a lift operator "a liftie" in Colorado, USA.

Linda's debut children's book *The Trick with Sticks* is written from the heart and inspired by the life experience of raising two children who have found social engagement challenging. She is passionate about helping children who find making friends and understanding the nuances of friendship a challenge. She hopes this book will empower everyone.

You can connect with Linda on:
facebook.com/lindacawley11
instagram.com/cawley.linda

ACKNOWLEDGEMENTS

Firstly, I want to say, I am so grateful to my beautiful family and friends.

In particular, and in no particular order, I would like to thank and acknowledge Heather Burzacott and Rachel James for being the first people I nervously read my story to, and even though my throat dried up and I was literally shaking, you were patient (once you got your coffee) and encouraging and supportive. Amanda McKean for your insightful perspective, highlighting that people who have a unique approach and can think differently is actually what the world desperately needs, and all differences are to be celebrated. Rachel Armstrong for your insight into how it feels when your friendships take off and when you make that connection. Ingrid Freriks for your tears; they made me feel like my message was really powerful. Mark Le Messurier, I was so nervous reading my story to you, but I knew if you thought my message could help others, then my story was compelling and potentially valuable to others. I appreciate your encouragement and support and for being the conduit to people who can help and guide. Cathy Domoney for being my cheerleader, for being there to answer my questions and for taking me through the process of self-publishing step by step. Your advice and guidance has been invaluable and has given me the confidence to go forth into what looked like quite an overwhelming process. My mother Brigitte Stanford for your helpful and considered edits.

To all the amazing teachers and carers who work tirelessly to help children with their difficulties in whatever field you may be. Know that you make a difference!

Thank you to my husband Tom, my daughter Grace and my son Austin. I wouldn't be me without you. Through all the ups and downs, we continue to learn and to grow.

Thank you to Grace for your beautiful illustrations and concepts. Your idea to make dogs the characters in this story was brilliant! Sometimes we can relate to dogs better than humans. I love your creative eye, your illustrations and all your ideas.

Thank you to Austin for listening and hanging on every word as I read the story to you. I love your encouragement and positive attitude.

Thank you to Tom for your time, energy, support and encouragement of the children and me. It was and always is limitless and amazing.

To our dog Molly for providing a footrest for me to lean on while I worked. I hope you like the portrayal of you in the story.

To everyone, please know that even the smallest act of kindness can make the biggest difference and impact.

www.ingramcontent.com/pod-product-compliance
Lightning Source LLC
Chambersburg PA
CBHW061357090426
42743CB00002B/47